Ezra Mundy Hunt

**Words about the War**

Plain Facts for Plain People

Ezra Mundy Hunt

**Words about the War**
*Plain Facts for Plain People*

ISBN/EAN: 9783337401993

Printed in Europe, USA, Canada, Australia, Japan

Cover: Foto ©ninafisch / pixelio.de

More available books at **www.hansebooks.com**

# WORDS ABOUT THE WAR:

## OR,

# Plain Facts for Plain People.

———◆•◆———

BY

## EZRA M. HUNT.

———

———

NEW YORK:

PRINTED BY F. SOMERSET.

No. 13 SPRUCE STREET.

1861.

# WORDS ABOUT THE WAR.

WITH every American citizen, and we might almost say, with every citizen of a free government, our present war is the subject occupying the largest share of worldly attention and remark. No ordinary times are these in which we live. Human society is disturbed to its foundations, and the greatest questions of national order and existence are in the process of agitation. No longer need we turn our eyes toward European struggles, and pass sentence upon the deeds of another continent. The crisis of the age is under consideration at home. It is not a time for day-dreaming, but life-acting ; not a period for doubtful disputations, but one when mind and men must with their reasons, opinions and acts throw the weight of their influence either upon the side of Liberty or Tyrany, of constitutional order and law, or of anarchy, confusion and misrule. It is vastly important that people of all classes and conditions should in this living present think and act aright, and not allow the interests of this or of coming generations to suffer damage by their delay. Right views are the parents of right action, and no earthly matter is at this time half so important as that the citizens of the country should be satisfied as to the causes that have brought about this war, as to the justness of our determined defence, and the results which are to be sought. Those who, under the first impulses of patriotism, have already recognized the great necessity of their decided co-operation and support of the Government in this war, need to know the facts bearing on the present struggle, that with calm and inflexible purpose they may be able to endure, if need be, prolonged effort, and occasional defeat. Those, on the other hand, who have little or no sympathy with the efforts put forth to suppress the rebellion, need kindly to be shown the justifying causes of our action, and to be induced to perceive that they occupy a position unjust to those who were the heroes of the revolution, unjust to themselves, and untrue to the great interests of American Liberty. Until I have exhausted all reasonable means to convince them I shall not denounce as traitors and tories those who are not lending the force of their influence to sustain us in this struggle.

Some have not enjoyed the means of information and cannot be expected to know the facts of the case, others have been misled by designing men, some are Nabals by nature, always in the negative on every other subject as well as this, some are self opinionated, and once getting an idea in their heads cling to it as their birth right, and have never been known to change on any subject whatever. The more closely facts and reason press upon them the more completely they close their minds to conviction, and even when silenced are true to the recipe of Hudibras,

> " A man convinced against his will
> Is of the same opinion still ."

Supposed political rules still bind those who have not yet learned that party is far below patriotism, and because they did not vote for the present officers they seem to feel they must sympathize with the enemies of our Government. But leaving out these scattered exceptions, it cannot be concealed that there are men among us, sensible and deservedly esteemed in other matters, who in one form or other fail to lend hearty co-operation in our present struggle. Some of them are professed Union men, but are crying "Peace, Peace, when there is no peace." They carp and criticize every act and measure of our chief officers for the suppression of the rebellion, and like Breckenridge councel a policy which, while pretending great respect for the Constitution, would, had it been pursued, left us ere this without one and the play and sport of faction and misrule. Others are timid, afraid that we shall not succeed, like those in Patrick Henry's time crying we are too weak, and magnifying every trouble and reverse. Others are in great fear as to its effect upon the times in the article of money, and are in real concern about the means of future support. Another class assume still more decided ground, and declare the war to be unjustifiable on our part, and to have arisen from a disposition to impose upon the South. These assert that she has not had her rights, and that she has due cause for this uprising and rebellion. We will suppose all these to be sincere, and, if so, open to kind conviction, and as such we shall address ourselves to them.

It is in no wise strange that such a party or parties should exist. War is in itself an evil, independent of necessity and of good results to be obtained thereby ; such an evil that the first impulse of men should be to avoid it. But when necessary, the law of self-preservation, the welfare of our country, of ourselves, of posterity, make it a thrilling, moving duty.

Even our own history has shown us the existence of such feelings. In the times of the glorious Revolution of '76 hundreds and thousands of American citizens, many of them good and substantial men, were opposed to the war. Sabine, the historian, says: "It is a very moderate computation to place the number of the Tories in the colonies who *in arms* aided the British troops, at 20,000. Thus a large share of the available fighting men in the colonies were arrayed against them. In the Carolinas and Pennsylvania the Whigs and Tories went through the war nearly equally divided. In Georgia the British held the State until 1782, and at the time of giving up, the royalist administration was complete throughout it. In New York the Loyalists were throughout the struggle the better party." One who will read the papers and correspondence of those times can not but see how many, who were no doubt sensible and good meaning men, disapproved of the Revolution, and yet many of them lived to bless its supporters ; and their children, in common with those of the patriots, have rejoiced with gratitude in the liberty thus secured. Is it not possible that you are making the same mistake? When posterity comes to pass judgment upon your opinions may they not stand astonished that you should have been idle or felt lukewarm amid such a struggle.

Come, let us reason together, and see the facts bearing upon the rebellion. None will deny but that for some cause, or under some pretense, certain of the States are resisting the authority of our Government. Under any and all circumstances *resistance* to a government must not only have reasons, but most weighty and unanswerable ones. "Prudence," says our Declaration of Independence, "will dictate that governments long established should not be changed for light and transient causes." Governments are not a mere idea. They are not the growth of a day or a year. Our Government was the result of four centuries preceding it. Like the Old English oak, if you cut it down it is many long years, if ever, before such another occupies its place. He who, without immense justification, lays hand upon a government commits a wholesale depredation upon the rights of man. It is "assault and battery" in its most diabolical proportion ; "highway robbery, with intent to kill," in its most daring audacity. Religion, philosophy, and law, have ever alike pronounced it among the foremost sins in the catalogue of crime. Our forefathers were able to enumerate, and by specific facts to show, at least twenty-seven distinct and flagrant reasons for their secession.

It is even a question whether under a republican form of government the right of rebellion exists at all. So long as its elections are conducted by law, its modes of representation maintained, the ballot box open, the supreme court unstained by a corrupt judicary, the same cause for rebellion can not exist as may in a monarchy where authority is not put to vote, but is an inherited, life-long power. Majorities limited by frequent expirations of their terms of office, with their powers modified by the different branches of government, and all in accordance with the laws of the Supreme Court, these are the ultimate reliances of our Liberty. If these do wrong for a time, the spread of virtue and intelligence, the changes of time, and the voice of public opinion will correct them. If these fail, our liberty fails, and the basis of our republican government is lost.

In such a land as ours the argument against rebellion is still further magnified. Other lands have rebelled against tyranny, but he who rebels against the American Government, rebels against the world's national standard-bearer of the banner of Liberty. Other rebellions have been in behalf of freedom ; this is in behalf of slavery. A government founded by men who with every advancing year have become more and more the admiration of the civilized world, whose wisdom and counsel drew forth eloquent plaudits from the Chathams and Burkes of the British Parliament, which have been more fully endorsed by orators and statesmen of every country and age, a constitution which has already been the model of one hundred and twenty more, a system which in its practical working has been found so efficient as to raise an infant republic in the short space of seventy years to a point scarce second to any nation on the globe ; such laws, such institutions, must have for resistance thereto, not only reasons, but such reasons as will carry home overwhelming conviction to the minds and consciences of a watching world. Posterity will ask of History enormous endurance, immense oppression, as the justifying causes of such rebellion.

It is not enough that little differences may have arisen, for happy families cannot always think just alike. It is not enough that interests have seemed to clash, and one is favoured at the expense of the other, for it is the beauty of our system that diffusion of knowledge, change of office, free discussion, and popular vote, provide a remedy for such friction, where a remedy is really needed or deserved. The highest justifying causes for rebellion under every system of free government are where the ballot-box is untrue, the courts corrupt, the voice of the majority unheeded, direct taxation oppressive, and access to the public ear prevented. None of these are claimed by any southern statesman, and all minor causes combined are not sufficient to make out a case justifying armed resistance. Besides, the history of our own Government has frequently shown how easily the voice of the people can be changed for due cause, how readily a wrong of one period, if it be a wrong, is corrected in another, and how time and experience give a changed view to human events.

In the formation of the Constitution, New York was the most fearful about her State Rights, instead of South Carolina. In 1814, New England was complaining of *sectionalism and oppression* instead of the South, and at the Hartford Convention actually adopted a resolution, "That the admission of new States into the Union, formed at pleasure in the western region, had destroyed the balance of power which existed among the original States, and deeply affected their interests."

The Protective Tariff was originally the policy of the South. Upon it Louisiana was dependent for her sugar culture, and still earlier, the culture of cotton was commenced only under its fostering care. The North was opposed to the system; and yet, in 1832, we find South Carolina endeavoring to rebel on account of it. The North accepts the system, and the South opposes it. Elections over and over again have shown precisely similar changes. States have been in turn the strongest on the side of one political party, and then of another ; and a single State, in the last election, changed its vote from that four years before, by one hundred and forty thousand. Surely, in view of such facts, rebellion, against any supposed grievance, is the most unjustifiable resort of the American people.

Resistence to such a government is so undeniably at war with all the principles of human and divine law, and has so little to excuse a crime, which has ever been classed among the most guilty and inexcusable in the conception of men, that even the very leaders of the movement seemed to have dreaded to face its enormity as treason.

In the history of government a new thing under the sun is claimed, and we have the so called " Right of *Secession.*" This means that our Government was so constituted that any State, whenever it may see proper, without the consent of the others or of the General Government, has a right to withdraw, and to be a separate country.

Let us see if it can not be proven, both from history and common sense, that such is not the case.

1. The first Union of these States was under the so-called " Articles of Confederation." The first sentence calls them "articles of confederation and perpetual union." Their title is in the same language. The words, *perpetual union*, are used five times in the document ; and surely *perpetual* did not in those days mean that a State

could leave whenever it sees proper.   The concluding part of its last
Article is this :

"Know ye that we, the undersigned delegates, by virtue of the power and authority to us given for that purpose, do, by these presents, in the name and in behalf of our respective constituents, fully and entirely ratify and confirm each and
every of the said Articles of Confederation and *Perpetual Union*, and all and singu-
lar the matters therein contained ; and we do further solemnly plight and engage
the faith of our respective constituents, that they shall abide by the determination
of the United States in Congress assembled, on all questions which by the said Confederation are submitted to them ; and that the articles thereof shall be inviolably
observed by the States we represent ; *and that the Union be perpetual.*'.

The preamble to our Constitution begins thus : "We the people of
the United States, in order to form a a *more perfect union.*"

The following points are undisputed matters of history.   Washington was among the first to feel the necessity of a Constitution, and
he took the first steps toward urging the matter upon the attention
of the proper authorities.   In a circular letter to the governors of the
States, dated June 8, 1783, he names as "essential to the existence
of the United States as an independent power, First, *an indissoluble
union* of the States under one federal head."   Surely, "never to be
dissolved," does not mean, to be dissolved at pleasure.

The Resolution, appointing the Convention to make our Constitution, in its preamble declares the design to be, "a firm national government.   It met in 1787.   Washington, President.   Governor Randolph, of Virginia, introduced the first series of resolutions by which,
as he said, he meant "a firm and consolidated Union."   Mr. C. Pinckney, of South Carolina, introduced a plan, as he said, "on the same
principles as of the above resolutions."   Mr. Patterson, of New Jersey, presented a plan, "on the basis of the sovereignty of the respective States."   Randolph's plan was adhered to.   Virginia, the Carolinas and Georgia, with other States, voted in favor of it.   The letter addressed, by unanimous order of the Convention, to the President
of Congress, has this language : "In all our deliberations on the subject, we have kept steadily in view the *consolidation of our union.*"

In answer to Hamilton's suggestion of its adoption by New York,
"with the reservation of the right to recede," Madison, a prominent
member of the Convention, and afterward a President, declares that
"the Constitution requires an adoption in toto and forever.   It has
been so adopted by the other States."

In the Legislature of South Carolina, in 1788, Charles C. Pinckney
her leading statesman said, "Let us consider all attempts to weaken
this Union, by maintaining that each State is separately and individ-
ually independent, as a species of political heresy which can never

benefit us, but may bring on us the most serious distresses." In 1789, South Carolina voted for "the firm consolidated Union." These are but a few of many like evidences to show that not only was our Government meant to be a perpetual Union, but that this right of secession was at that very time discussed and decided against, and that decision is our Constitution. It was meant to make of the United States a nation. Hence we have ever talked of our national welfare, interests, and institutions. It was reserved for the disciples of Calhoun to start the doctrine that this is a grand mistake, and to say, as did General Quitman, who until his death was the next representative of this doctrine, "that the United States is not, nor never has been, in any true sense a nation."

Now look at a few of the absurdities of the so-called right of secession.

If one State has a right to secede, so have all; and then where is the Government, and who pays the debts?

If secession is a right, New Jersey, or any central State, may secede, and invite some European power to her borders; and then who shall protect the other States?

If the Constitution gives the right of secession, then it is the spectacle of a government making provision for its own destruction. Was this the wisdom of our fathers?

Would we have ever paid what, at our present population, is equivalent to 400,000,000 of dollars for Florida, Texas, Louisiana, and the country west and northwest thereof, if we believed they had the right to leave whenever they chose?

Such, briefly yet sufficiently, is the truth of history and of common sense as to this so-called right of secession; and yet Davis and his confederates profess not to be rebelling, but seceding. Neither history nor reason can find the distinction. It is treason in lamb's-wool. It is what the leaders themselves *have not claimed the right of*, and that is rebellion.

We have then before us the fact, that a portion of the country is disobeying the Government, setting at naught its authority, and disregarding its laws. In seeking out the enormous reasons which should in any way justify such a proceeding, it is right and fair first to turn to the leaders of the outbreak, and hear what they have to say in justification.

In the list of grievances mention is made of the Tariff. It was in reference to this that South Carolina, in 1832, espoused the doctrine of Nullification, and assumed a right to set at naught the revenue laws of the United States. The larger portion of the South was suffering, as they supposed, from the unjust oppression of this tariff; but here again we learn how little excuse these sectional views are for disturbing the peace of the Union. A single passage from the speech of A. II. Stephens, of Georgia, now Vice-President of the so called Southern Confederation, disposes of the whole matter:

In 1832, when I was in college, South Carolina was ready to nullify or secede from the Union on this account. And what have we seen? The tariff no longer distracts the public councils. Reason has triumphed. The present tariff was voted for by Massachusetts and South Carolina. The lion and the lamb lay down together; every man in the Senate and House from Massachusetts and South Carolina, I think, voted for it, as did my honorable friend himself. And if it be true, to use the figure of speech of my honorable friend, that every man in the North that works in iron, and brass, and wood has his muscle strengthened by the protection of the Government, that stimulant was given by his vote, and I believe every other Southern man. So we ought not to complain of that. [Mr. Toombs —That tariff lessened the duties.] Yes; and Massachusetts with unanimity voted with the South to lessen them, and they were made just as low as Southern men asked them to be, and that is the rates they are now at. If reason and argument, with experience, produced such changes in the sentiments of Massachusetts from 1832 to 1857 on the subject of the tariff, may not like changes be effected there by the same means—reason and argument, and appeals to patriotism—on the present vexed question? And who can say that by 1875 or 1890 Massachusetts may not vote with South Carolina and Georgia upon all those questions which now distract the country and threaten its peace and existence? I believe in the power and efficiency of truth, in the omnipotence of truth, and its ultimate triumph when properly wielded.

Something has been said by way of complaint by one or more Southern statesmen about the fishing bounty and the navigation laws. If there is reason for complaint at all, the West has far more occasion as to these than the South; but Stephens and Everett, between them, have set these matters at rest. Stephens shows that they were commenced under a Southern President, and not a single administration has ever set "its principles or policy against them." Everett shows that it amounted to but $200,005 as an annual average, and in the single matter of removing the Indians from Georgia more money was expended than for fishing bounties in seventy years. As to the navigation laws, the prince of Southern statesmen says that "they were commenced under one of the Southern Presidents, and had been continued through all of them since," and that the effort of his friend Mr. Toombs to get them repealed "had met with but little favor North *or South*."

Texas, in her ordinance, gives one original cause of secession, and that is, she has not been "properly protected on her exposed frontier," when she has cost us more than a hundred million of dollars, and the chief expense of our military department has been of the Southwestern frontier. As a comment upon this reason, you need but to have seen the care-worn troops who were so meanly betrayed after her revolt. But all these are mere incidental points. Throughout the South, and chiefly throughout the North, the subject of Slavery is in some form or other the alleged reason for this rebellion. Gathering up all the general or specific charges which are to be found in Southern conventions, journals, Congressional reports, and excited speeches, from the time of the first agitation until last November, they are all included under these four reasons:

I. The election of a Republican President.
II. The agitation of the Slavery question.
III. The limitation of Slavery extension.
IV. Disregard of the Fugitive Slave Law.

I. Is the election of Mr. Lincoln sufficient cause for rebellion against the authority of this Government? It is admitted that his election was constitutional; that it was by a fairly expressed vote, in a contest into which North and South, East and West entered; by what the Constitution regards as a majority, in a word; that in mode and form of nomination and election there was nothing contrary to our laws. The objection is not to the mode.

Is it to the man? He was by all the forms of the Constitution in every way eligible to the office. He was not one who had rendered himself especially obnoxious to the Southern States. A Kentuckian by birth, and a Western man by settlement, he had never identified himself with those sections of which the South has mostly complained. No inflammatory speeches or sarcastic denunciations had ever escaped from his lips. During the canvass he did not express himself in any way hostile to Southern interests. Yet he was not a man whose views were unknown. They had been most severely tested by Mr. Douglas but two years before, without reference to this election, and had undergone no change whatever. These two questions had then been distinctly asked him, and in writing he had answered them:

*Q.* I desire to know whether Lincoln to-day stands, as he did in 1854, in favor of the unconditional repeal of the Fugitive Slave Law?

*A.* I do not now, nor ever did, stand in favor of the unconditional repeal of the Fugitive Slave Law.

*Q.* I want to know whether he stands to-day pledged to the abolition of Slavery in the District of Columbia?

*A.* I do not stand to-day pledged to the abolition of Slavery in the District or Columbia.

He had added to these the following remarks:

As to the first one, in regard to the Fugitive Slave Law, I have never hesitated to say, and I do not now hesitate to say, that I think, under the Constitution of the

United States, the people of the Southern States are entitled to a Congressional Fugitive Slave Law. Having said that, I have had nothing to say in regard to the existing Fugitive Slave Law, further than that I think it should have been framed as to be free from some of the objections that pertain to it, *without lessening its efficiency.* And inasmuch as we are not now in an agitation in regard to an alteration or modification of that law, I would not be the man to introduce it as a new subject of agitation upon the general question of Slavery.

The second one is in regard to the abolition of Slavery in the District of Columbia. In relation to that, I have my mind very distinctly made up. I should be exceedingly glad to see Slavery abolished in the District of Columbia. I believe that Congress possesses the constitutional power to abolish it. Yet, as a member of Congress, I should not, with my present views, be in favor of *endeavoring* to abolish Slavery in the District of Columbia, unless it would be upon these conditions : *First,* that the abolition should be gradual ; *second,* that it should be on a vote of the majority of qualified voters in the District ; and *third,* that compensation should be made to unwilling owners.

He was nominated as a conservative man, whose character and conduct had been that of thoughtful honesty rather than that of impetuous ambition. He had expressed the opinion that slavery ought not to be allowed in the Territories of the United States, but had in no way argued anything but an entire silence on the part of the Government in respect to it as in the States.

Was it the party who elected him ? They had a right to express their opinions by their votes, or even their choice, where they had but few opinions. Thousands who voted for him differed on some points from the Republican party. It of itself was but a recent party, and our history had often before shown that the result of one election was no criterion for the next. The same papers which announced their success also declared "an anti-Republican majority in both Houses of Congress." The platform of the party had this resolution thus plainly expressed :

That the maintenance inviolate of the rights of the States, and especially the right of each State to order and control its own domestic institutions according to its own judgment exclusively, is essential to that balance of powers on which the perfection and endurance of our political fabric depends ; and we denounce the lawless invasion by armed force of the soil of any State or Territory, no matter under what pretext, as among the gravest of crimes.

There was an actual gain of anti-Republicans in Congress, showing that other causes had operated besides this one question in his election. Besides, as we shall see more fully hereafter, the result had actually been brought about by the conduct of the Southern States themselves. The language of Mr. Stephens on these points is not only of force, because from him, but because it is the language of common sense and fact. In his Georgia address, November 14th, 1860, he says :

Are we entirely blameless in this matter, my countrymen? I give it to you as my opinion that but for the policy the Southern people pursued, this fearful result would not have occurred.

Had the South stood firmly in the Convention at Charleston, on her old platform of principles of non intervention, there is in my mind but little doubt that whoever might have been the candidate of the National Democratic party would have been elected by as large a majority as that which elected Mr. Buchanan or Mr. Pierce. Therefore, let us not be hasty and rash in our action, especially if the result be attributable at all to ourselves.

In my judgment the election of no man, constitutionally chosen to that high office, is sufficient cause for any State to separate from the Union. It ought to stand by and aid still in maintaining the Constitution of the country. To make a point of resistance to the Government, to withdraw from it because a man has been constitutionally elected, puts us in the wrong. We are pledged to maintain the Constitution. Many of us have sworn to support it. Can we, therefore, for the mere election of a man to the Presidency, and that, too, in accordance with the prescribed forms of the Constitution, make a point of resistance to the Government without becoming the breakers of that sacred instrument ourselves? Withdraw ourselves from it? Would we not be in the wrong? Whatever fate is to befall this country, let it never be laid to the charge of the people of the South, and especially to the people of Georgia, that *we* were untrue to *our* national engagements. Let the fault and the wrong rest upon others. If all our hopes are to be blasted, if the Republic is to go down, let us be found to the last moment standing on the deck, with the flag of the Constitution of the United States waving over our heads. Let the fanatics of the North break the Constitution, if such is their fell purpose. Let the responsibility be upon them. I shall speak more presently of their acts. But let not the South, let us not be the ones to commit the aggression. We went into the election with this people. The result was different from what we wished; but the election has been constitutionally held. Were we to make a point of resistance to the Government, and go out of the Union on that account, the record would be made up hereafter against us.

I do not anticipate that Mr. Lincoln will do anything to jeopard our safety or security, whatever may be his spirit to do it ; for he is bound by the constitutional checks which are thrown around him, which at this time render him powerless to do any great mischief. This shows the wisdom of our system. The President of the United States is no emperor, no dictator he is clothed with no absolute power. He can do nothing unless he is backed by power in Congress. The House of Representatives is largely in the majority against him. In the very face and teeth of the heavy majority which he has obtained in the Northern States, there have been large gains in the House of Representatives to the Conservative Constitutional party of the country, which here I will call the National Democratic party, because that is the cognomen it has at the North. There are twelve of this party elected from New York to the next Congress, I believe. In the present House there are but four, I think. In Pennsylvania, New Jersey, Ohio, and Indiana there have been gains. In the present Congress there were 113 Republicans, when it takes 117 to make a majority. The gains of the Democratic party in Pennsylvania, Ohio, New Jersey, New York, Indiana, and other States, notwithstanding its distractions, have been enough to make a majority of nearly thirty in the next House against Mr. Lincoln. Even in Boston, Mr. Burlingame, one of the noted leaders of the fanatics of that section, has been defeated, and a conservative man returned in his stead. Is this the time, then, to apprehend that Mr. Lincoln, with this large majority in the House of Representatives against him, can carry out any of his constitutional principles in that body? In the Senate he will also be powerless. There will be a majority of four against him. This after the loss of Bigler. Fitch. and others, by the unfortunate dissensions of the National Democratic party in their States. Mr. Lincoln can not appoint an officer without the consent of the Senate—he can not form a cabinet without the same consent. He will be in the condition of George the Third (the embodiment of Toryism), who had to ask the Whigs to appoint his ministers, and was compelled to receive a cabinet utterly opposed to his views. And so Mr. Lincoln will be compelled to ask of the Senate to choose for him a cabinet, if the democracy of that body choose to put him on such terms. He will be compelled to do this or let the Government stop, if the National Democratic men (for that is their name at the North), the conservative men in the Senate, should so determine. Then how can Mr. Lincoln obtain a cabinet which would aid him, or allow him to violate the Constitution? Why, then, I say, should we disrupt the ties of this Union, when his hands are tied, when he can do nothing against us?

It is said he was elected by a section or by a sectional party. This is not strictly true. The South has no right to call itself one section, and all the other States another. We have the Eastern, Middle, and Western States, as recognized sections, often with interests quite diverse. Buchanan did not obtain a single electoral vote in New England, yet the cry of sectionalism was not raised. The States North had each large parties opposed to Lincoln, and divided between Douglas, Breckenridge, and Bell. New Jersey at least did not deserve to be called sectional. The States South did not all vote in the same way, but differed among themselves. In fact, the question of sections has nothing to do with such an election. Our fathers wisely left this matter to regulate itself. It always has in the past, and will in the future. New England has ceased complaining of the sectionalism of the West, and the West ceased so shrilly to cry for internal improvement. It seems to me that all of us, with Stephens and Douglas, Breckenridge and Everett, Holt, Dickerson, and Dix, and with the Republicans themselves, must agree that the mere election of Lincoln did not justify rebellion—is not the shadow of an excuse for defiance to such a government as ours.

II. The agitation of the Slavery question is assigned as another cause for rebellion. 1. To be of any force as a reason for breaking up the Government, the South must needs prove that the entire responsibility of this rests with the other sections. But what are the facts? Our Government started with slavery excluded by common consent north of the line of the Ohio River, and it was not until it was attempted to introduce slavery into Missouri, that the agitation commenced. In position, in character, in cultivation, it resembled the

States formed from the Northwest Territory. The plea of extreme heat, or of the necessities of the cotton crop, did not here apply. From all the territory we had acquired by purchase, one Southern State, Louisiana, had already been admitted as slave, and freedom was at least entitled to a share. If you will review the discussions on this subject for the last forty years, it is plain to perceive that the Hotspurs of the South were not excelled by the most ultra of the North. Interference with freedom commenced on the one part before interference with slavery on the other. They who make unreasonable demands, not those that resist them, first deserve the name of agitators.

2. It must be shown that this agitation has injured the South. But what are the asserted facts? Senator Hammond, or Gov. Hammond, of South Carolina, October 26, 1858, in discussing the advantage this agitation had been to the South, speaks of the " happy results of the abolition discussion. So far," says he, " our gains have been im; mense from this contest, savage and malignant as it has been." Then as to the value of negroes, we know this has nearly doubled within a few years. Here again is his testimony : " In this very quarter of a century our slaves have doubled in numbers, and each slave has more than doubled in value." " My deliberate judgment," says Stephens. in January, 1857, is, that "by these agitations, slavery has been greatly strengthened and fortified—strengthened and fortified not only in the opinions, convictions, and consciences of men, *but by the action of the* Government." One who has visited the South can not but receive the same impression. So far as the agitation has been in reference to the extension of slavery, the fact is that the South has not and can not have slaves to extend it with, unless the African slave-trade is resumed. The increase, rapid as it is, is not rapid enough to supply the home demand. Again; this slave agitation has been chiefly fostered by acquisition of new territory, and this has been eminently Southern policy. Our Government has paid millions for States now slave, where it has but thousands for those free.

3. This agitation was not even on the increase. The fact is, that so far as the main question is concerned, that of slavery in the States, the country has for years been tending to a more settled and satisfactory policy. In 1836, petitions were signed by thousands and tens of thousands for the prohibition of slavery in the District of Columbia, and in all the forts, dock-yards, etc., of Government, while multitudes advocated general emancipation ; but now such views are not pressed in our Government. The Abolitionists themselves have felt increasing weakness as to numbers—have denounced as traitors states-

men whom they once thought sympathized with them, and admit themselves to be a very small party. The testimony of Democratic and even of Southern governors of Kansas, and that of the investigating committee, have proved, beyond the shadow of a doubt, that here the great error was on the side of slavery, and that such wrongs as were then attempted ought to be agitated.

4. But the chief point is this. Mere agitation is a miserable excuse for breaking up so glorious a government as ours. If wrong, it is not wrong enough for that. It has brought forth no destruction to any part of our land, and with the records of our own history the South should be the last to complain. She asked for slavery in Louisiana, and she got it; in Florida, and it is granted; for the annexation of Texas, with the privilege of four more States to be carved therefrom, and she obtained it; for New Mexico, and she had it; for Missouri, and she had it; for a Fugitive Slave Law, the most stringent of any property law on our record, and she obtained it; for the repeal of the Missouri Compromise, and she got it; for the doctrine that the Constitution carries slavery into the Territories, and the courts attempted so to decide it. But once in the history of our Government has it without compromise decided opposite to Southern view, and that was the admission of Kansas. Surely such facts might excuse the North for complaint, but never the South for rebellion.

III. Another reason assigned for rebellion is the limitation of slavery extension. This, in fact, is the only significance of the election of Lincoln. But his choice does not even settle this. When we remember that he was chosen over three opposing candidates, the opposition thus being scattered and disorganized, that thousands voted for him who do not fully subscribe even the platform of the party; that it was with multitudes rather the expression of their displeasure at the repeal of the Missouri Compromise, than a desire for universal restriction; and that the election of congressmen, which is full as much an expression of sentiment, was just in the other direction, we see the folly of such an excuse. It did not even settle this matter against Southern sentiment. It was but a four years' choice, and not sustained by congressional aid. No case was at hand, or likely to be, upon which to act. If Southern rights were jeoparded at all, it was in mere theory, not in fact. In a popular government all can not be expected to think alike, and for a minority to rebel, is treason in the start. A part of Pennsylvania once felt just as sorely under Washington, all New England under Madison in 1814, and South Carolina under Jackson in 1832, and yet on these points each has been relieved. These almost prophetic words of Henry Clay, in 1850, are still the true language of common sense.

Mr. President : I am ready to say, that if Congress were to attach within the States the institution of Slavery for the purpose of its overthrow or extinction, my voice would be for war. But if the two portions of this Confederacy should unhappily be involved in civil war, in which the effort on the one side would be to restrain the introduction of slavery into new Territories, and on the other side to force its introduction there, what a spectacle would we present to the contemplation of astonished mankind ! An effort not to propagate right, but I must say an effort to propagate wrong. It would be a war in which we would have no sympathy, no good wishes, and in which all mankind would be against us, and in which our own history itself would be against us. The Government has no right to touch the institution within the States ; but whether she has, and to what extent she has the right or not to touch it outside the States, is a question which is debatable, but which, decided however it may be decided, furnishes, in my judgment, no just occasion for breaking up this happy and glorious Union of ours.

IV. A fourth, and the only remaining reason assigned, is a disregard of the Fugitive Slave Law.

The Constitution does provide that a " person at service or labor in one State fleeing into another, shall be delivered up on claim of the owner." Now to the facts of the case. There is no law on any statute-book of the land for the fulfilment of which such provisions have been made. Most stringent, and in some cases severe measures have been adopted by the General Government to secure its execution. States took the matter into their own hands, until a decision of the Supreme Court which has never been suspected of conniving at any neglect of Southern rights, decided that it was the business of the Federal Government, by its officers in the several States, to see to its execution. Facts and history testify how diligently they have attended to their work. The law has been faithfully executed. In vain have such men as Douglas and others called upon the South to cite an exception. It is true that in some cases there has been difficulty, but it has not been between the South and the Federal Government, but between the Government and individuals of the North, and in behalf of the South, and the Government has always triumphed. In the case of the slave Jerry, at Syracuse, in the midst of excitement, and in a region most hostile to the institution of slavery, still the right of the Government to rescue, triumphed. Authorities do not furnish a single exception. Our treasury has borne the cost of the enforcement of the law. The rights of trial by jury have been waived. slaves returned on what in common law would have been doubtful evidence, and " free men been sent to the South as slaves who have been returned on our hands." There are good laws against murder, yet too often the murderer escapes ; there are laws against burglary and theft, and yet these occur; but so long as law makes an effort for justice, we do not complain of its occasional failure, much less rebel against all law.  It is a fact, as plain as recorded facts can make it, that no class of people in the land have—where they have made effort and proved ownership—succeeded so well in reclaiming stolen or strayed property, as have the South.

Another point: The evil to require rebellion should be on the increase.  Here are the statistics of the census of 1860 and of 1850, showing a decided decrease in this suppose cause of offense.

FUGITIVE SLAVES AS RETURNED BY THE SEVENTH CENSUS (1850) AND THE EIGHTH CENSUS (1860) RESPECTIVELY.

| STATES. | Slaves. | CENSUS OF 1850. Fugitives. | One in | Slaves. | CENSUS OF 1860. Fugitives. | One in |
|---|---|---|---|---|---|---|
| Alabama | 342,814 | 29 | 11,822 | 435,132 | 36 | 12,087 |
| Arkansas | 47,100 | 21 | 2,224 | 111,104 | 28 | 3,868 |
| Delaware | 2,200 | 26 | 88 | 1,798 | 12 | 160 |
| Florida | 39,310 | 18 | 2,184 | 61,753 | 11 | 5,614 |
| Georgia | 381,682 | 89 | 4,288 | 463,230 | 23 | 20,096 |
| Kentucky | 210,981 | 96 | 2,698 | 225,490 | 119 | 1,895 |
| Louisiana | 244,809 | 90 | 2,726 | 332,520 | 46 | 7,228 |
| Maryland | 90,368 | 279 | 314 | 87,182 | 115 | 758 |
| Mississippi | 309,878 | 41 | 7,558 | 436,696 | 68 | 6,422 |
| Missouri | 87,422 | 61 | 1,457 | 114,965 | 99 | 1,161 |
| North Carolina | 288,548 | 61 | 4,508 | 311,108 | 61 | 5,263 |
| South Carolina | 384,984 | 16 | 24,061 | 402,541 | 23 | 17,501 |
| Tennessee | 239,459 | 70 | 3,421 | 275,784 | 29 | 9,543 |
| Texas | 58,161 | 29 | 2,005 | 180,388 | 16 | 11,274 |
| Virginia | 472,528 | 83 | 5,693 | 490,887 | 142 | 4,195 |
| Totals | 3,200,364 | 1,011 | 3,165 | 3,919,557 | 803 | 4,911 |

Even of these, numbers escape to the Everglades of Florida, or to the wild wildernesses of some dismal swamp.

Another point: The complaint is chiefly from States that seldom or ever have a fugitive escape to the North.  South Carolina is loudest in the cry, and gives this, in her secession ordinance, as the reason for her rebellion; yet it is not probable that five Carolina negroes can be found in all the Northern States, and Canada besides. As was said by Douglas in one of his last speeches in the Senate, "Kentucky and Illinois can see no cause for separation on this account."  It is South Carolina and Vermont that have the greatest gratuitous excitement about the whole affair.  Never was a government more faithful to its obligations than has been ours in this respect.  It has seemed to be the hobby of our Supreme Court to give the most strict construction to the law, and the highest ambition of our federal officers to enforce it.  The Virginia slave escaping to Maryland was returned by the same process as the one escaping to Pennsylvania.  In neither case were State officers called upon to carry out the provisions of the law.  Any refusal on the part of

States to co-operate, if unfriendly, was not unconstitutional, and in no case successful.

But it is affirmed, and that truly, that some States have enacted laws at variance with the requisitions of the Fugitive Slave Law. But have these, in any single case, prevented the carrying out of the provisions of the United States law. Not one. If these laws are at variance, is not the proper course to draw the attention of the General Government to their correction? Yet this has never been done in the form either of resolution in Congress or of appeal to the Supreme Court. But even the facts as to the existence of such laws have been misrepresented. Not a single border State (and these are the ones to which fugitive slaves mostly escape) has a law at variance with the United States law on this point. Ohio, Indiana, Illinois, Minnesota, California, and Oregon have, we believe, no laws in force on the subject. New Jersey has had no trouble about the matter, so far as we know, within the memory of the oldest inhabitant. Pennsylvania has not legislated directly upon the law of 1850, has not closed her jails against fugitives, and has no provision in conflict with the United States law. The very last case under it was a triumphant vindication of the law. "The State of New York has passed no laws having relation to the United States Fugitive Slave Act of 1850. Though pressed frequently upon the Legislature, they have always failed of adoption." Rhode Island had a law not constitutional, but at the suggestion of her noble governor it was repealed when first complaint was made thereof. In fact, the ablest article prepared upon these laws shows that only Vermont, Michigan, and Wisconsin have laws on this point unconstitutional, and they are, as such, null and void. Wherever, in tested cases, slaveholders have failed in recovering their property, it has been in cases where they have not established an ownership, or have in some way been defeated in due process of a friendly law. Their success has been more uniform than that which has attached to lawsuits generally.

Besides, are there no laws or acts on the part of the South that are equally as unconstitutional. The same article and section of the Constitution which requires the return of fugitives says: "The citizens of each State shall be entitled to all privileges and immunities of citizens in the several States." Has the Supreme Court labored to enforce this as it has the Fugitive Slave Law? Are there any commissioners in the several States to fulfil its provisions? Has Judge Lynch, who for so many years has dispensed law liberally at the South, ever been tried for unconstitutionality? From the case of Judge Hoar to the present time, have there not been numberless

instances of restriction on civil privileges? Senator Johnson tells us
that the terms of citizenship are such, in South Carolina, as to property,
that there he never could have had a vote, much less been a Senator.

"No two months," says B. F. Butler, "have passed, in the last ten years at least,
in which outrages have not been committed upon Northern men in the South,
which, had they been perpetrated by a foreign nation, would have demanded a
redress of grievances under pain of a suspension of diplomatic relations. But we
have borne these outrages because there was no tribunal to the arbitrament of
which we could submit them, and it was against the genius of our people to appeal
to arms."

We complain, not that the abolitionist should be hardly dealt with
at the South, but cases are known to myself, and numberless ones
have been well authenticated, where, even in previous years, unof-
fending and prudent men have been assailed and maltreated, and
great encroachments made upon human liberty. Had an American
citizen abroad been treated as many a one has at the South on mali-
cious suspicion, the whole force of our Government would have been
threatened for his protection.

Perfect justice can not always be attained in small communities,
and less in a wide-spread nation, but a government which has so in-
dustriously tried and so efficiently succeeded in sustaining a law
which must be expected not to excite the admiration of all, deserves
anything but rebellion and attempted destruction at the hands of
those whom it has so diligently protected.

From the summary of the pretended, we now turn to the real
causes of this rebellion. They are three:

I. An over-indulgence of the South by the North.

II. A change of view on the part of leading Southern men on the
subject of slavery.

III. The wrong feeling and wrong action which the continuous
existence of slavery in a republic is sure to beget.

Let us follow up the history of the Government from the formation
of the Constitution until the present time, and see how plainly pure
facts prove these positions.

I. As to over-indulgence. 1. The mode of representation adopted
in the very start, although not so intended, has had this effect. If
the prominent doctrine now advocated by the South is true, that
the slave is to be dealt with as property, then why should the man
worth five thousand dollars by virtue of holding five slaves have, in
representation in Congress, three votes therefore besides his own,
while I, worth just as much in other stock, have nothing but my own
single count? Look at the great advantage and indulgence thus
secured.

It takes 91,935 white men and women North to secure one representative in Congress, but only 68,726 South. Nearly half of the delegation from South Carolina occupy their seats by virtue of their negro population. This representation of what they call property, and of what are not certainly citizens, has furnished the South a majority sufficient to carry its measures. We have not had the chance to impose if we would. The representation by States, instead of by population, gives 13,238,670 people North, only as many Senators as 6,186,477 had from the South. Thus, in both halls of Congress, 6,186,477 white people South have 120 representatives, while 13,238,670 North have but 176. The ratio by numbers would be 246, i. e., about 20 more than we have. These are according to the last census, and our recent one shows a still greater increase. I need not follow out the vast advantage the South has possessed by this arrangement.

2. This indulgence is manifest in the whole history of our legislation and politics. The Government began with slavery, by direct law, excluded from all the territory it owned. Under the next head we shall easily show that no such idea as the further extension of slavery ever entered the minds of those who formed our Constitution and procured our liberties. Yet the chief policy of our Government has ever been controlled by the South and by slave-interests. When a Tariff, and a United States Bank, and the policy of Internal Improvements were advocated there, they succeeded, and when not, they failed. When Louisiana Territory was wanted at $15,000,000, though the country was still poor in means, it was purchased. Florida was obtained at five millions of dollars, and eighty millions more spent in wars to rid it from its aboriginal inhabitants. Southern immigrants secured the independence of Texas, and as a Southern policy it was annexed to us, and the result was an expenditure of $210,000,000. All this out of the mutual treasury, and paid for Southern policy, with not a dollar to balance it for the North. The after-expenses of protecting the frontier more than balanced any local benefit of ours. Our wars with the English, the Indians, and the Mexicans were all at the bidding of Southern statesmen. New England uttered her protest, but sent her sailors to secure the victory; and away off in unfriendly Mexico, notwithstanding distance and climate, we furnished one third of the soldiers, and more than half of the two most trying things for war, the money and the deaths.

"Five hundred million dollars of the public funds," says Everett, "of which, at least, five sixths have been levied by indirect taxation from the North and Northwest, have been expended for the Gulf States in this century." The policy of the South has been, almost invariably, the policy of the country. How could it be otherwise? By her slave-property representation, she ever had such a majority as was sufficient to turn the scale in her favor. Where questions of slavery extension were involved, she has, in every case where the States themselves had not already decided the matter, been able to triumph as to the Territories. New Mexico, throughout whose plains and mountains the government of Mexico had issued a proclamation of liberty and a law against slavery, again has it permitted under a more enlightened government. When, in 1836, the question of the abolition of slavery and the slave-trade in the District of Columbia was in agitation, the House of Representatives adopted, at Southern desire, the following resolution by a large majority:

*Resolved*, "That all petitions, memorials, and resolutions, propositions or papers relating in any way or to any extent whatever to the subject of slavery or the abolition of slavery shall, without being either printed or referred, be laid upon the table, and that no further action whatever shall be had thereon."

It is the only instance in our history where the right of petition was ever denied, and remained thus on the statute book till 1845, when, out of respect to the general right, it was rescinded. Upon complaint that anti-slavery papers had been sent South, permission was also given to search the mails and burn the matter.

In almost every party and political move, the question of availability has been discussed, and this has usually meant what will be acceptable to the South. In fact, so used had we become to this sense of governmental inferiority, that we have been in the habit of introducing Southern gentlemen as something more than ordinary Americans, and they themselves, in Europe, have learned to quote themselves as from the South rather than from the United States in general.

This over-indulgence or permitted balance of power has been equally manifest in official appointments. Look over the record from the beginning of our Government until that of the present rebellion, a period of nearly seventy-two years. Twelve out of eighteen Presidents have been Southerners, and have held office forty-eight years, or over two thirds of the time. Besides, Pierce or Buchanan would not be accused of any sectional proclivities toward the North. The Secretaries of State have been fourteen from the South to nine from the North, or forty years out of sixty-nine.

The Speakers of the House have been forty-five years Southern men, twenty-five Northern.

The Presidents *pro tem.* of the Senate have, since 1809, all been from the South, except Southard and Bright, and these for but a short time. Jesse D. Bright was as true then to his Southern bias as he is now.

Seventeen out of twenty-eight Judges of the Supreme Court have been Southerners, and a majority always.

Eighty out of 134 Foreign Ministers have been from the South.

"Of 307 principal appointments under the Constitution, 204 have been held by slaveholders." When we take into view the more than twofold population of the North, and her greater advance in science and education, the disproportion shows an enormous favoritism.

A single fact from our Post-office statistics shows how we have indulged the South in a pecuniary point of view. According to the tables for 1859, the postage collected in the Free States was $5,532,999, and the expense of carrying the mails $6,748,189, leaving a deficit of $1,215,189.

In the Slave States the amount collected was only $1,988,050, and the expenses of carrying the mails $6,016,612, leaving the enormous deficit of $4,028,568. The Slave States did not pay one third of the expense of carrying their mails, and Massachusetts, besides paying for hers, had a surplus larger than the whole amount collected in South Carolina.

II. The second cause of this difficulty is the change of view which has occurred in the South in reference to slavery. For the sake of brevity, I shall subjoin, without extended comment, specimen extracts from present and former statesmen. They will of themselves prove this wondrous backsliding of view, and show that it is the South, not the North, that is so changed as to slavery—

GEORGE WASHINGTON: "There is not a man living who wishes more sincerely than I do to see a plan adopted for the abolition of it. But there is only one proper and effectual mode by which it can be accomplished, and this is by legislative authority."

PATRICK HENRY: "Slavery is detested—we feel its fatal effects—we deplore it with all the earnestness of humanity."

THOMAS JEFFERSON: "When the measure of their tears shall be full, doubtless a God of justice will awaken to their distress, and by diffusing a light and liberality among their oppressors, or at length by his exterminating thunder, manifest his attention to things of this world."

JAMES MADISON: "We thought it wrong to admit in the Constitution the idea that there could be property in men."

JOHN RANDOLPH, 1820: "Sir, I envy neither the heart nor the head of that man from the North who rises here to defend slavery on principle."

Hon. Mr. REID, of Georgia, 1820: "Slavery is an unnatural state, a dark cloud which obscures half the lustre of our free institutions."

1832, in the Legislature of Virginia, Mr. BOLLING, of Buckingham County: "That slavery is an evil, a great and appalling evil, I dare believe no sane man could or would deny. That it is a blighting, withering curse upon this land is clearly demonstrated by this very discussion itself."

Mr. CHANDLER, of Norfolk: "I took occasion to observe that I believed the people of Norfolk County would rejoice, could they, even in the vista of time, see some scheme for the gradual removal of this curse from our land."

Mr. FAULKNER, of Berkeley: "The idea of a gradual emancipation and removal of the slaves from this Commonwealth is coeval with the declaration of your independence of the British yoke. Slavery, it is admitted, is an evil."

Gov. McDOWELL: "It has been frankly and unequivocally declared from the very commencement of this debate, by the most decided enemies of abolition themselves, as well as by others, that this property is an evil—that it is a dangerous property."

Judge E. IREDELL, of North Carolina: "When the entire abolition of slavery takes place, it will be an event which must be pleasing to every generous mind."

Such are the correct reflections of the general sentiment of the South during the earlier years of our history. They recognized slavery as an existing evil, were sorry for its presence, and while they did not feel that the General Government should interfere with it in the States, they had not yet come to behold it as a blessed institution. But how changed now the modes of expression and the language of debate! Evil habits indulged in either by good men or bad, too soon come to lose their hideous hue, and from being tolerated, grow at length to be enjoyed. We now find the first men of the South speaking of it through these many years, not as an evil to be deplored, but a glorious institution to be encouraged.

Let us commence with the grand high priest of this changed Southern view.

JOHN C. CALHOUN: "Slavery is the most safe and stable basis for free institutions in the world."

JEFFERSON DAVIS: "It is but a form of civil government for those who are not fit to govern themselves." He evidently now proposes to extend the application of his original idea over the North.

HUNTER, of Virginia: "It is the normal condition of human society, beneficial to the non-slaveowner as it is to the slaveowner — best for the happiness of both races." "The very keystone of the mighty arch which, by its concentrated strength, is able to sustain our social superstructure, consists in the black marble block of African slavery."

Senator MASON, of Virginia : "Slavery is ennobling to the master, elevating to the slave."

Dr. PALMER, of New Orleans : "The mission of the South is to conserve and perpetuate the institution of domestic slavery as it now exists."

Senator IVERSON, of Georgia : "Slavery must be maintained—in the Union, if possible; out of, if necessary; peaceably if we may, forcibly if we must."

Senator BROWN, of Mississippi : "I want Cuba. I want Tamaulipas, Potosi, and one or two other Mexican states ; and I want them all for the same reason—for the planting and spreading of slavery. I would spread the blessings of slavery, like the religion of our Divine Master, to the uttermost ends of the earth ; and rebellious and wicked as the Yankees have been, I would even extend it to them."

Mr. GAULDEN, of Georgia, an able member of the Charleston Convention : "I believe slavery right, morally, religiously, socially, and politically. Let us ask our Northern friends to give us all our rights, and take off the ruthless restrictions which cut off the supply of slaves from foreign lands. The African slave-trader is the true Union man. I believe he is a true missionary. I tell you the slave-trading of Virginia is more immoral, more unchristian, in every possible point of view, than the African slave-trade, which goes to Africa and brings a heathen and worthless man here, makes him a useful man, and sends him and his posterity down the stream of time to join in the blessings of civilization."

Quotations "*ad nauseam*" might, as you well know, be added from the Wises, Pryors, Wigfalls, Thornwells, and Rhetts of the South, from governors and legislators, judges and courts—in fact, from every department in which leading Southern men are found—to show that too extensively there has been a sad change in Southern sentiment. The testimony of two prominent men to this point is sufficient, if any more evidence is needed.

Governor and Senator HAMMOND, of South Carolina, says (October 24, 1858) :

And what *then* [1833] was the state of opinion at the South? Washington had emancipated his slaves. Jefferson had bitterly denounced the system, and had done all he could to destroy it. Our Clays, Marshalls, Crawfords, and many other prominent Southern men led off in the colonization scheme. The inevitable effect on the South was, that she believed slavery to be an evil—weakness, disgraceful, nay, a sin. She shrunk from the discussion of it. She cowered under every threat. She attempted to apologize, to excuse herself on the plea—which was true—that England had forced it upon her. But now it would be difficult to find a Southern man who feels the system to be the slightest burden on his conscience, who does not, in fact, regard it as an equal advantage to the master and slave, elevating both as to wealth, strength, and power, and as one of the main pillars and controlling influences of modern civilization, and who is not now prepared to maintain it at every hazard.

ALEX. H. STEPHENS, of Georgia—speech at Savannah, March 21, 1861:

The prevailing ideas entertained by Jefferson and most of the leading statesmen, at the time of the formation of the old Constitution, were that the enslavement of the African was in violation of the laws of nature—that it was wrong in principle, socially, morally, and politically. It was an evil they knew not well how to deal with ; but the general opinion of the men of that day was that, somehow or other, in the order of Providence, the institution would be evanescent, and pass away. This idea, though not incorporated in the Constitution, was the prevailing idea at the time.

Our new government is founded upon exactly the opposite ideas. Its foundations are laid ; its corner-stone rests upon the great truth that the negro is not equal to the white man. Our new government is the first in the history of the world based upon the great physical, philosophical, and moral truth. Many who hear me perhaps can recollect well that this truth was not generally admitted, even within their day. The errors of the past generation still clung to many, as late as twenty years ago. This stone, which was rejected by the first *builders*, is become the chief stone of the corner in our new edifice.

Here is proof better than pages of argument as to who have changed on this great question. The policy of our forefathers was by a limitation of the African slave-trade, by preventing introduction of new slaves, and by preventing its spread to new territories, thus to cause the system to circumscribe itself and become extinct. The policy of the South—that which has brought upon us our present evils—has been to extend the so-called beneficent institution as far as their power and influence could carry it. The whole tendency of this admitted change of sentiment has been to promote agitation, to encourage demands at variance with the design of the Constitution, as it is admitted to be at variance with the will of its founders, and then to call those agitators who oppose these new doctrines. It is a party which thus, by their own admissions and assertions, have been for the last thirty years breaking in upon the principles of our forefathers, and then, in order to shelter themselves, accuse those who have resisted their encroachments of creating an excitement and endangering the liberties of the country.

**III.** The third cause of the present war is the wrong feeling and wrong action which are inseparable from the continuous existence of slavery in a republic.

This was most fully recognized by the founders of our Government. Slavery then existed in all but one of the States, and those who formed the Constitution, and who were members of our earlier legislative bodies, knew its workings.

JEFFERSON, in the full vigor of his intellect, had well depicted its true results in a national point of view. Speaking of the conduct of masters toward their slaves, he says:

The parent storms ; the child looks on, catches the lineaments of wrath, puts on the same airs in the circle of smaller slaves, gives loose to his worst passions, and thus nursed, educated, and daily exercised in tyranny, can not but be stamped by it with odious peculiarities. The man must be a prodigy who can retain his manners and morals undepraved by such circumstances. And with what exceration should the statesman be loaded who, permitting one half of the citizens thus to trample on the rights of the other, transforms those into despots, these into enemies, destroys the morals of the one part and the *amor patriæ* or love of country of the other.

With the morals of the people their industry is also destroyed—for in a warm climate no man will labor for himself who can make another labor for him. This is so true, that of the proprietors of slaves a very small proportion indeed are ever seen to labor. And can the liberties of a nation be thought secure when we have removed their only firm basis—a conviction in the minds of the people that these liberties are the gift of God? that they are not to be violated but with his wrath ?

It is not that the people of the South are in any way by nature debased, but no class or nation can withstand such bad influences. Where they are recognized and deplored as evils they are, like sin to the Christian, unfruitful, but yet not so debasing ; but where these very things are rejoiced in, the eyes are shut to watchfulness, and the evil ranges in its unrestrained degradation. The man who, as a system, can make others work for him without any pay, who can live on the hard toil of others alone, who can buy and sell for money men, women, and children, often by necessity without any regard to the family relation, who, as the unlimited monarch of 20, 50, 100, or 500 negroes, can use or abuse them as he chooses, and yet feel no desire for times when such things shall be at an end, has in the very process a training which unfits him or his posterity for aiding in a free government permanently.

There is no true democracy in such training. It is all aristocracy. There is no republicanism here. It is slavery. There is no appreciation of the rights of the working classes. It is the one prominent idea of self-superiority. The lord of the plantation, with the additional power and swell of rank added to him, thus gets so in the habit of feeling big, that it does not subside even at Washington.

Knowledge, virtue, and a sense of the dignity of labor are the three great starting-points in the success of a republican government, and none of these are fostered by slavery. The very system places each of them at a discount.

Education would kill slavery, for every man South and North knows that if you educate a man he will not work for nothing, as a system. The necessary habits, mode of life, training, and surroundings of slavery do not foster religion in either master or slave; and Jefferson has exhausted the other point when he says that "in a warm climate no man will labor for himself who can make another labor for him." It is not that every slaveholder is a bad man, for circumstances, natural ability, some peculiar powers of parental training, and the grace of God make exceptions; but one not, by personal residence and the laws of habit, contaminated or habituated to the influence can not fail to perceive that the practices of slavery are not the school for the purest knowledge, the best morals, or the most energetic industry; not the place to learn how to dispense laws to a free people, or how to be governed by the voice of a constitutional majority. Submission to the ballot-box, to the jury, to the law, is a lesson the master never learns at home. His biggest, longest, fullest lesson, from early childhood to decrepit age, is, *Submission to me*, and that is a poor lesson to be so forcibly taught in a republican government. Did space permit, many arguments and a thousand facts in our actual history might be adduced as to these points; but my object is rather to show the key which opens up the causes of our trouble, and to lead others to follow on to their own legitimate conclusions. Actual occurrences in our Government, in our halls of Congress, and in public acts have so clearly demonstrated these points as scarce to need rehearsal; and the present war is but the ripe fruit dropping from this upas-tree, which from a little shrub has been growing up under the shadow of our tree of liberty. The hope, dawning bright through the future, is that this is the last crop; that now, at least, in some way, a final settlement will be made.

We have thus briefly noticed what Secession or Rebellion is, and what are its assumed and its real causes. To one who will honestly follow the history of our Government, from the times when our fathers fought, and bled, and died in its defense, to those in which we live, and will but read and see the facts of our political history, the bare-faced iniquity of this whole rebellion can not but be apparent. It has never, in its enormity, had a parallel since the revolt of

Satan from the authority of Heaven. The stream of ancient and of modern history has no such muddy pool in its midst. As the mind rests after its vain search for causes justifying the enormity of such an outbreak, it can but sadly sigh over the new insight into human wickedness thus uncovered. But the practical question right at hand is, What is to be done? There can be but one reasonable answer. The rebellion must be put down. It is no time for hesitating on minor points. The actual existence of our Government is involved; our personal liberties are assailed; the interest of human civilization, and liberty, and law, and morals are all on trial in the conflict. They take a narrow view of the whole matter who regard it as a small difference, to be all settled up in a few days. We live in an epoch and era of history. There have been heretofore some years in the world's history that in their weighty results have counted large as centuries, and so shall it be with our day. For weal or woe we are deciding the rights of constitutional law to maintain itself, the power of free institutions as a form of government, and the condition of the generations who may follow us in the line of posterity. If we hesitate now, the grand armada of popular rights and boasted independence goes down amid the howling storm, and the black night of the most exciting anarchy that ever registered its name in the chronology of history. If in the nineteenth century of the world's life the United States of America are to be dissolved by an armed rebellion, seeking to break over all its noble constitutional laws, and to found an empire avowedly resting upon a principle of slavery, then well may we forever bid a last adieu to all anticipations of earthly peace, and consider the "rights of the people" forever hereafter the name for a baseless shadow. But no, it is not so—so it shall not be. The Government must be sustained. When my house is attacked and my home interests are in peril, I care not in whose charge it may have been placed, I will go and defend it. Now is not the time for us to talk of party or power. The Supreme authority—that is our Government, and it must be supported so long as it is evidently making honest effort to subdue the rebellion. They who are constantly finding fault with little matters should be willing to feel that these are of but little consequence compared with the great issue at stake. Madison said, in 1789, " No man but an enemy of liberty will stand on technicalities and forms when the essence is in question." Mistakes will undoubtedly be made; but we do not sustain our best friends in the time of their peril by expanding their little faults, even though they be real, but rather by standing up firmly as their unswerving friends. The United States Government, the best earthly friend of every American citizen, has now the right to just such support from you. The Republican should sustain the war, not merely because of his opinion or vote, but because a rebellion has occurred—because the Constitution and laws are assailed—because an armed force is attempting to go contrary to the government of that "perpetual Union" which was formed for "ourselves and posterity."

The Union man should sustain the war, not only because the very name of his party declares him opposed at all hazards to a separation, but because the very Constitution which he has so loved as to be satisfied with it just as it is, is broken and made as a thing of naught; and most of all, the Democrat should support the war because he, of all others, is the most outraged by this attempt. His very name denotes his belief in the right of majorities to govern. His very name is the oath of submission to the expressed will of the people. His very name denotes his opposition to an aristocracy of wealth or even to any system of labor which does not secure to all the right of reward therefor.

Besides these, there are certain facts in connection with this war which should make the Democrat incensed beyond all other men at the action of the South. It has been the party which has ever been faithful to the so-called rights of the South; which has given them its chief appointments; which has for them suffered in many things, and which, when united, still had at the North a powerful organization. The principle of the Democratic party has ever been submission to the will of the majority, and yet in disregard to this very principle, a part of the party has forsaken the other. Besides, the whole conduct of the Charleston Convention, so far as the South was concerned, was in utter disregard of all Democratic principles. The question was not, what is the will of the majority? but will the whole party submit to the will of the few? Still more flagrant is the fact, that the South departed from the old platform, and asked more than ever before. Noble men contended that the principles of Democracy were unchangeable, and that they should make their stand upon the Cincinnati platform, which left the Territories equally open to settlement from every section. But this was not enough. The South had in our early history acquiesced in the exclusion of slavery from every particle of our territory; had then consented to its exclusion only south of the line 36° 30′, but had now not only succeeded in repealing the Missouri Compromise, but was actually contending that the Constitution carries slavery into the Territories, and some absolutely denied the right of a State to apply for admission with slavery excluded. In a speech made at Augusta, Georgia, Sept. 1st, 1860, A. H. Stephens clearly exposes the faithlessness of the Southern Democracy Speaking of the secession or withdrawal of delegates from the conventions at Charleston and Baltimore, he says :

This secession movement is founded on a departure from principle, not only a departure from the Georgia platform, and from the long established principles of the National Democratic party, but upon an entire change of position of the entire South of all parties, not of all individuals, in relation to the power and jurisdiction of the Federal Government over the subject of African slavery. What I affirm is, that the position of the South for twenty years and more—since the celebrated Atherton resolutions—has been a denial of the jurisdiction of Congress over the subject of slavery in the States and Territories. It was upon this denial of jurisdiction that the South resisted the reception of abolition petitions. This position is directly reversed at Charleston and Baltimore. If we go to Congress with a request, a petition, or demand to pass a law to protect slavery in the Territories, why may not—on the same principle, so far as jurisdiction of the question is concerned—the anti-slavery men of the North go before the same body with their request, petition, or demand, and ask that such a law shall not be passed, or that one of a contrary character shall be passed?

November 14, 1860, he says, in remarks on the election of Lincoln :

I give it to you as my opinion, that but for the policy the Southern people pursued, this fearful result would not have occurred. Had the South stood firmly in the Convention at Charleston on her old platform of principles of non-intervention, there is in my mind but little doubt that whoever might have been the candidate of the National Democratic party, would have been elected by as large a majority as that which elected Mr. Buchanan or Mr. Pierce.

When I review the records of that Charleston and Baltimore Convention, and behold the utter unreasonableness of Southern men, I wonder not that General Butler, who there plead for union on the good old platform, should have seen enough to nerve him to draw the sword against such fanatics, as that thousands and tens of thousands who know the history of their betrayal, should with indignant earnestness resolve to maintain our rights to the last. Against such an exacting oligarchy it was in vain that then their best friends plead for a return to reason, and where such men as Butler, Buchanan, Cass, Douglas, Dix, Dickinson, Holt, and a host of other names distinguished on the Democratic roll, bid you at all hazards to throw the whole weight of your power and influence in the scale of our Government, you need not hesitate. Events even then as well as now showed that there was no spirit of conciliation or compromise on their part. Yancey, the leader of the crew, had said long before this : " By one organized, concerted action, we can precipitate the Cotton States into a revolution."

A Democratic administration used every means in their power to avert the storm, or even to postpone it, but while our princes plead,

the Confederates robbed our Government and fired upon our vessels,
and assumed the attitude of bold revolt. "A committee," says
General Dix, "of which I was chairman, in an address to our Southern brethren, adopted at a meeting in Pine Street, in December la i
recommended that the States should meet together for consultation,
and if they could not settle their difficulties amicably, and preserve
the Union, that they should arrange the terms of separation, and
save the country from the horrors of civil war. We implored them
to pause in order to give us time for an effort to restore harmony
and fraternal feeling. We appealed to them in language of entreaty,
which would have been humiliating if it had not been addressed to
brethren of the same political family. To this appeal, enforced by
the concurrence of eminent citizens of this State, who had always
been the most strenuous advocates of Southern rights, the States to
which it was addressed responded by setting the authority of the
Union at defiance, by seizing the public forts and arsenals, by seducing
Federal officers from their allegiance, and in one instance by confiscating the treasures of the Government. For months these outrages
were submitted to, with no effort on the part of the Government to
resent or punish them, in the hope that, under the guidance of better
counsels, those who committed them would return to their allegiance."
They sent us commissioners, not to arrange terms of conciliation, but
of separation—not to unite, but to dissever our country. The sug-
gestions of Buchanan and of Lincoln as to a convention of all th.
States were alike totally disregarded on their part, although acquiesced in by the North. The attempted peace conventions were crip
pled by the absence of representatives from the States most con
cerned, and yet even these showed a disposition to restore the
Missouri Compromise, to make fully effective the Fugitive Slave
Law, and to provide in the Constitution for complete non-intervention
with slavery in the States. But the Cotton States did not wait for
terms of peace. That was not what they desired. In their imagina
tions they had already builded a tower of Southern independence, an
ideal republic, with the negro as its foundation, cotton its support,
and aristocracy its king, and the blind infatuation was not to be
restrained by any appeals to argument or fact. Our only resort is
an "appeal to arms and to that God who presides over the destinies
of nations," and who is upon the side of the right. In one sense, it
matters little as to the causes of the war, for when the house is on
fire, the point is to put it out, rather than to stand parleying as to
the method of its start; but when, as in this case, we come to exam-
ine the high-handed treason of this rebellion, it can not but nerve our

energies and incite our zeal. When under the guidance of the master spirit of this rebellion, South Carolina raised her arm of resistance, swearing "by the Eternal," the noble Jackson said, "Our Federal Union—it must be preserved." Nullification was secession in the bud, and he blighted it. It was resistance of one national law. Secession is resistance to them all, and the occasion for decision thus multiplied by the greater enormity and extent of the offense requires us to grapple with the monster, though it be a lion grown. It is either a life or death struggle for free governments everywhere. Interests immense enough to thrill every frame with concentrated, working, praying, giving energy, are at stake in the issue. Let not a hand falter, not a heart hesitate, not a man be lukewarm in such a struggle. By all the justice of sublime right, by all the value of our blood-purchased liberties, by all the enormity of this uncalled-for rebellion, you are summoned to use to the uttermost all the means and influences necessary to victory. Your country, your family, your posterity, and freedom all over the great world has a claim upon your persistent, unflinching, untiring devotion to this cause. The man who in such a crisis will stand balancing himself hither and thither amid mere party issues, shows that he has not nobility enough to rise to the higher level of patriotic devotion. What we now want is not Politics, but Patriotism. Let the old lines be blotted out, and let us now know but one party, and that our country's; or if we must have two, let it be plainly those who contend for a vigorous prosecution of the war, without any idea of a dissolution of the Union, and on the other hand, those who are willing to purchase peace at any price.

We proceed last to inquire as to the results of this war. No one a single year since would have predicated the state of affairs now existing, and no one can fully define the results of events at present transpiring. A few thoughts, however, in reference to them are well to be kept before the mind.

To many the cost of the present war and the hard times connected therewith are the first prominent matters of thought. Yet as to both of these there are hopeful views. New England sighed over the war of 1814 as ruining all her interests, and at the time it did indeed cause suffering and want, but it proved one of the grandest elements in her subsequent success, and her commerce and manufactures, her material interests, owe more to that war than to any one cause of progress. War employs labor and capital; it sets in circulation the gold and silver which has not been accessible to the poor. Its tendency is to equalize wealth. The rich, by our system of taxation, contribute far more in proportion than the poor, and I am greatly disappointed if the effect of this war will not be greatly to benefit the laboring classes. As to its cost, when not so rich we expended over 500,000,000 of dollars, chiefly for Southern lands and defenses, and we are as able to spend at least such an amount in defense of our liberties. How a country can endure the expense of war we can only learn from the records of the past, and he who will study English or French history, and then compare the ability of our country at present with these in former days, will not be distressed as to our resources. The little property of thirteen colonies, that could endure the expense of a seven years' war with England in '76, will not, in its present developed state, be troubled by a calculation of expense. In a single week the call for investment on behalf of the Government has been met by a response of millions of dollars. Such a country need have no fear as to the materials for prosecuting the war.

II. A result to be sought in this war is a re-modeling of our political habits. We have before us the demonstration that " knowledge and virtue are necessary to perpetuate our independence." We must re-write the motto, not only on the portals and domes of our liberty temples, but in the hearts and consciences of our people. In the South, one out of twelve of the white population can neither read nor write, besides the tens of thousands for whom little attempt is made, and who yet are represented in the councils of the nation. At the North, knowledge and religion do not prevail as they might, and the whole land needs more of education, industry, and morality. Bible principle and general intelligence must be made to take their place as the foundations of our Government. Good men must not allow themselves to be thrust aside by pot-house politicians, but must take their places in the primary meeting, or in whatever is the starting-point of legislation. So long as the man who can neither read nor write, or who comes reeling to the ballot-box, is allowed his vote, so long as it is no crime for men to purchase votes and office, so long as intelligence and morality are at a discount in high places, so long republican forms of government must be a failure. Certain facts and phases of American society and morals trouble me more than burnished guns and glistening bayonets across the Potomac ; and in the grand re-construction which must eventually take place if our country is restored, we must now begin to lay again the foundation of liberty in morals, education, and justice. This is not the work of resolve, but of time, and now is the time for the capable and the good to take their places in the primary work of redeeming the land from the traitorship of politics. Although this war may take time and money and human lives, yet all will be well expended if they serve to cleanse away the filth of party organization and bring us back again to the purity and principle of earlier days. Some other system than packed conventions and political bribes must furnish our legislative counsels with proper representation. Delegates to nominating conventions must be voted for at the same time our representatives are chosen, or some other plan must be adopted completely to overturn the wire-pulling clique-work of the land. If slavery was the nest-egg of this rebellion, politics has hatched it—and it is proving itself the befitting progeny of such a pedigree.

III. Another result to be sought is the final settlement of this vexed slavery question. Different views, in this respect, will undoubtedly prevail. One class will be willing, in order to have peace, that slavery be allowed to run, have free course, and be glorified, and thus will consent to purchase peace by the sacrifice of principle, and present ease at the immense cost of prospective punishment and misrule. Another class will be satisfied that the States shall be brought back as before, with the prevention of the African slave-trade, and the non-extension of slavery forever determined; willing to let it remain as it is in the States, hoping that, notwithstanding the fact that vice has never been known to die out by being left alone, and, notwithstanding slavery, even in the States, has been actually on the increase, that yet in some way or other it will cease to exist. They will thus be satisfied to leave this matter to time, believing that the reorganization of society, and the new colonization which will inevitably ensue from the present war, as well as the new sources of supply for the products of slave-labor which will be found, will of themselves destroy the system. A third class, few and small, will cry for immediate emancipation as the only cure of all our troubles.

A fourth will take the ground, that so long as we perpetuate the cause of our troubles, and a system which, in itself, has a tendency to unfit men for participating in a republican government, we can have no permanent peace; that now is the time to provide for the complete extinction of this system, not by any unjust act, but by confiscating this as well as other property of rebels, and by purchasing of those not rebels, their slaves, or by so setting bounds to the system as that for the public good it shall cease, after a specified period, under an equitable system of compensation. A fifth will feel that it is enough to know that the existence of our nation is at stake, and that one and all should unite to subdue the rebellion, leaving all questions formerly at issue between us to be settled either by the

Constitution or by a Convention, called in accordance with its provisions. Such seems to be the plain doctrine of the present Administration. We are not yet able fully to discern what may be the indications of Providence, of reason, and of statesmanship, but such points as these should be undergoing the careful scrutiny of human mind, in order that we may act right at the right time, and secure a perpetual liberty to us and to our children. It is a time for the American people—the masses—to be thinking as well as acting. A chip can float, but a nation, as well as a man, is tested by being equal to emergencies. We must open our minds to a more adequate conception of the immense, unparalleled interests which cluster around the age—around us. To live in such a crisis and be equal to it is a grand glory—to stand trembling, hesitating, or drawing back is a misfortune sadder than oblivion. Let us set up no false banners.

If we are fighting for the existence of our Government, for the supremacy of law, for our Republic, that is grand enough. So let it nerve the heart and strengthen the arm.

If, besides the great problem of the possibility of stability in republican forms of government any and everywhere is under trial, still more immense and intense is the struggle. If so, let a watching world inspire us.

If, whether we will or no, the condition and destiny of another race is involved, let philanthropy utter its voices, and let us seek what is duty here. There are interests, it may be, pending, worthy of the manly courage and heroic endurance of many a year. Our country, posterity, humanity, and God, it may be, have claims upon us which can not be discharged in a single campaign.

We have nothing to fear so much as a patched-up peace. From the time of Jeremiah to that of John Breckenridge, it has ever been the resort of traitors, no less than the faint-hearted, to cry for peace when there is no peace. The recent letter of General Butler has the true sentiment on that point:

I see with pain upon the part of some of those with whom I have acted in political organizations a disposition to advocate peaceful settlements, wherein there can be no peace. However desirable, it is not to be purchased on any terms save the recognition of the authority of the Federal Government over every inch of territory which ever belonged to it. A peace involving the separation of the Union, or until the supremacy of the Government is forever established, would be simply a declaration of perpetual war of sections.

Let us nobly face the music of constitutional liberty, and defend the rights of our Government, until they who have attempted to trample upon its institutions shall be ready to seek an honorable peace at our hands. As a nation, we have sinned in egotism, in extravagance, in political corruption, and in derelictions from principle, but our sin is not imposition upon the South. We had endured until submission had almost ceased to be a virtue, but now that, still worse, the hand of war is raised against us, it is time to arise to the full demand of·our civil, political, and moral rights. The war will be short enough, when it ends with these secured.

Not permitted myself to engage in armed defense of that country whose present welfare is so near my heart, I have thus endeavored to present a few considerations worthy of our attention in the present crisis. I can not believe that the numbers who are not fully aroused with a sense of justice and of duty in the present struggle are aware of the facts of the case, for all history can not make out a clearer defense than can the American citizen for a hearty co-operation in the support of this war. I have purposely avoided elaborate argument or pathetic appeal, that I might present in brief, facts which can not but carry conviction to the honest heart. Up to the time of the Charleston Convention a Democrat in politics, descended, like the Southerner, from the Cavaliers whom some one meanly describes as "gentlemen adventurers, aspiring to live by their own wits," born and bred in the moderate, conservative State of New Jersey, and by a Southern sojourn and acquaintanceship having seen Southern society and institutions, with liberal allowance, my mind was not cheerfully brought to the sad realities of our present peril. But history, and acts and facts which I can not resist any more than I can a belief in the simplest axioms of truth, force me, as I believe they will you, to an unreserved dedication and determination, founded upon the full persuasion that it is our duty, one and all, with one heart and one mind, throwing aside all other political issues, to fight and work and labor on manfully, energetically, patriotically, unflinchingly, until the arm of rebellion is paralyzed, and the power of this best of all governments fully re-established.

I shall, in conclusion, add to this, as expressing the true sentiment which should fill every American heart, the following eloquent language from the mouth of D. S. DICKINSON :

I hold it to be the first duty of every citizen, of every party, to aid in restoring if restored it can be—this great and good Government. If it is right for a portion of this country to take up arms against this Government, it is right to sustain such action ; and if they are wrong, they should be put down by the power of the people. There is no half-way house in this matter--no tarrying-place between sustaining the Government and attempting its overthrow. There is no peace proposition that will suit the case until the rebellion is first put down. ° ° I believe this rebellion did not arise out of sectional agitation, but from a blind, wicked, reckless ambition. And I believe it is the duty of every man, woman, and child to raise an arm against it to crush it.  ᵒ  ᵒ  Those causes of irritation, although they may have suggested to Southern States to request becoming guaranties, they never justified armed rebellion in any shape or manner. And what were those causes of irritation? The only real, practical cause of irritation was the non-execution of the Fugitive Slave Law. But that did not affect the Cotton States, so called ; but Missouri, Kentucky, Virginia, Maryland, and Delaware, and perhaps one or two other States, were the only ones ever injured by it. The Cotton States, so called, never lost a fugitive slave from the time of their existence to this day. To be sure, they had a question about territories, but it was so entirely ideal, a mere abstraction, and so practically not a real grievance. But if it had been, they had the Supreme Court and both branches of Congress, and practically had control of the question. The fugitive slave question was the only practical question which annoyed them, and that question was not the cause of the rebellion. What State first seceded ? South Carolina began to scrape lint before the votes were counted. She had no practical grievance whatsover.  ᵒ  ᵒ  I was for negotiating a peace, until a fortification was fired upon by rebel artillery, and then I bade adieu to all expectations of peace until conquered over rebellion. I say there is no peace until you can put down rebellion by force of arms ; and when every other man, woman, and child in the United States has acknowledged the independence of the revolted States, to those with arms in their hands I will still oppose it, and I will talk for my own gratification when no others will hear me. We must stand by the Union. Fellow-citizens, the language of Andrew Jackson was, "The Union must and shall be preserved." What would Gen. Jackson have done had he been at the helm to-day ? He would have hung the traitors higher than Haman. You may make peace with the loyal men of the South, and there is the place to make it. But how will you do it with rebellion ? Go with an agreement in one hand and a revolver in the other, and ask the Confederacy to take its choice ? If there is any you can deal with, it is the loyal citizens of the South—those that are persecuted for the sake of their Government—those that love their Constitution, and are willing to die in its defense, when they are restored to position by conquering rebellion. Are you in favor of war ? No ; but I am in favor of putting down war by force of arms. I am opposed to war, and in favor of obtaining peace by putting down the authors of the war. I am in favor of peace, but I am in favor of the only course that will insure it—driving out armed rebellion, negotiating with loyalty. We must fight battles, and bloody battles. We must call vast numbers of men into the field. We must not go as boys to a general training, with ladies, and idlers, and members of Congress to see the show, but we must go in earnest—go prepared for action—to fight it as a battle, and not to fight it as a play-spell. We must unite as a whole people, going shoulder to shoulder. And when we do so, we shall conquer. And why ? We have the right, we have the prestige of government, have the sympathy of the disinterested world, we have the moral and material elements to do it all, and to insure victory. Rebellion has not the financial ability to stand a long war, with all their gains from privateering and piracy, and issuing Confederate bonds—made a lien upon the property of people who were never consulted as to their issue, and who repudiate them—worth as much as a June frost, a cold wolf track, which no financier fit to be outside of the lunatic asylum would give a shilling a peck for. They may vex, they may harass, they may destroy, they may commit piracy, but the reckoning is to come for all this. They will be brought to the judgment of the American people—of their own people. They will be a: raigned, and who is there will be ready to stand up as their defenders in the name of the Constitution?    *    *    It will be time enough to struggle over who shall administer the Government when we are sure we have one to administer. He who is not for it, is against it. I have determined to fight this battle out, but on no political grounds. I stand upon the constitutional ground of my fathers. There I will stand, and animate my countrymen to stand with me : and when once we shall have peace restored—when we shall have put down rebellion, when we shall have encouraged fidelity, when peace and prosperity shall again greet us, then let us see if any part of any State is oppressed, if any individual is wronged, if any are deprived of their rights—see that equal and exact justice is extended to all.

www.ingramcontent.com/pod-product-compliance
Lightning Source LLC
Chambersburg PA
CBHW032143080426
42733CB00008B/1178